WHO NEEDS STORIES?

Traditional tales retold by
Kimberley Reynolds
Series Advisor Professor Kimberley Reynolds
Illustrated by Diego Moscato

OXFORD
UNIVERSITY PRESS

Letter from the Author

I grew up in a big family in the United States of America. I had four sisters, a brother and lots of pets, including a goat. We all loved children's books. (The goat liked eating them!) Sometimes my mother had to declare there would be 'no reading at the table' to  remind us to talk to each other. When I moved to England, I discovered I could study children's books at university. Now I teach children's literature at Newcastle University.

The stories in this collection have travelled over time and space. *The North Wind and the Sun* is one of the fables told by the slave Aesop who lived in Ancient Greece. *The Monkey and the Crocodile* comes from the *Panchatantra*, a collection of tales from India written about two thousand years ago. To me both stories still seem funny and wise. I hope you agree!

Kimberley Reynolds

Once, a storyteller came upon a town where people never told stories.

'Why do we need stories?' they asked. 'We like facts, and we get them from the Internet.'

'You can get stories on the Internet, too,' said the storyteller.

'What use are stories?' the people asked.

'What use are stories?' cried the storyteller. 'They make you think! They help you solve problems! You need stories to help you understand how the world works!'

But the people just laughed.

The storyteller knew that somehow she needed to bring stories back to the town. While she was thinking about how to do it, she heard unhappy voices coming from a nearby park. She saw a group of children huddled together.

'What's the matter?' she asked them.

'We always play in this park,' answered a boy. 'But today a new group of kids have decided that they're in charge. They've taken over the swings and the slides. They keep telling us what to do.'

5

'Yes,' complained one of the girls. 'There are more of us so we should be in charge. We should make them do as we say.'

'But how?' said the others. 'Shall we fight them?'

'Crick crack,' said the storyteller.

'You need to use your brains, not your fists.
I know a story that might help.'

'How can a story stop bullies?' grumbled
the children.

'Let's see,' said the storyteller, and she
began to tell the story of ...

The North Wind and the Sun

A long time ago, when the world was still young, North Wind woke up feeling cross. It made him want to show everyone how big and powerful he was. He puffed up his cheeks and began to blow. Soon the grass and flowers began to bend and sway.
North Wind blew harder.

Branches broke off trees and roofs flew off houses. All this blowing made him feel huge and powerful.

'Look what I can do,' he boasted to Sun. 'All you do is hang in the sky, but just feel me blow.'

North Wind blew again and made the sea rise up angrily. He made huge waves and smashed ships onto rocks.

Sun watched the destruction, and knew he must find a way to stop North Wind.

Far below, he spotted a man walking along a road, and he had an idea.

'North Wind!' he shouted over the noise of the gale. 'You make a lot of noise, but I am more powerful than you.'

'Prove it,' demanded North Wind.

'Do you see that man in his winter coat?' asked Sun.

'I see him,' said North Wind.

'Let's see which of us can make him take his coat off,' Sun declared.

'That's easy,' said North Wind, hurling a blast of freezing air at the man. 'I'll blow his coat off him.'

North Wind blew and blew. But, as the air grew colder and the Wind became stronger, the man frowned and wrapped his coat more firmly around himself. He pulled down his hat, and stuck his hands in his pockets. North Wind blew even harder.

The man snuggled deeper into his coat and carried on walking. North Wind was angry now. He blew up a gale. The man bent his head and pushed on.

At last, North Wind grew tired from all his blowing. 'I give up,' he puffed.

'My turn,' said Sun.

As he felt the Sun's warmth, the man began to smile. Soon he took his hands out of his pockets.

Sun shone harder and the man removed his hat and wiped his brow. Walking was making him hot. Before long, he took off his coat!

When he saw what Sun had done, North Wind realized that he had made a mistake. 'I'm sorry, Sun,' he said to his old friend.

'I don't know why I was in such a temper. It was just a big waste of energy! But I think I'd better blow just a little now because that poor man looks as if he's far too hot!'

And so, they worked together, the Wind blowing gently and the Sun shining. The man went on his way, thinking what a strange but beautiful day it had been.

'Hey!' said a boy. 'That story has given me an idea. We don't want to fight the others. We want to be like the Sun and *persuade* them to play.'

In no time, they had started a game of chase in and out of the trees.

The sound of their laughter drew the bigger children from the play equipment, and soon they joined in, forgetting all about bossing the others around.

'Well, that's one thing stories are good for,' the storyteller thought as she watched them. Then she set off to find a place to stay.

The storyteller was kept busy in the town without stories. Wherever she went, there was a situation that called for a story. One afternoon, she came across a little girl who was crying her eyes out because her best friend had played a mean trick on her.

'Crick crack,' said the storyteller. 'What use are stories if they can't show friends how to fix an argument? Do you want to hear what happened when one friend tricked another?'

The little girl sniffed and nodded, as the storyteller began the story of ...

The Monkey and the Crocodile

Long ago, when animals could talk and all
creatures were friends, the two best friends of
all were Monkey and Crocodile. Monkey lived by
himself, and the things he liked most in the world
were talking to Crocodile and eating the sweet
berries that grew at the very top of the trees.

Every morning, Monkey would climb to the
jungle canopy to gather the ripest berries. They
tasted as sweet as sugar. He picked all the
berries he could carry, then he waited for Crocodile
to swim over from his nest in the middle
of the river. They spent each afternoon
chatting and sharing the berries.

Crocodile had a sweet tooth. He loved the berries as much as he loved Monkey, and he loved Monkey almost as much as he loved his wife.

Every afternoon, Crocodile left his wife sitting on the forty eggs she had laid. Then he swam over to tell Monkey about the forty fine little ones that would soon hatch. As they talked, Monkey would toss sweet berries down to Crocodile, who snapped them up greedily.

Monkey could never carry enough berries to satisfy Crocodile. Although Crocodile always promised his wife that he would bring her some berries, he never managed to stop himself from eating them all!

It wasn't just his love of the sweet berries that stopped Crocodile keeping his promise. Crocodile had no pockets, so he had to carry the berries in his mouth. As he swam home, the sweetness of the berries filled his mouth, and before he knew it he had swallowed them all down in a great, delicious gulp.

His wife was very unhappy. 'Here I sit all day and all night, waiting for our eggs to hatch, and you can't do me this one little favour. I don't believe you love me at all,' she wept one morning. 'If you did, you would bring me some of those sweet berries.' With that she wrapped her tail around her eggs and pointed her snout in the air.

Crocodile told Monkey his problem. Because he was so fond of Crocodile, clever Monkey thought hard. He thought and he thought, and suddenly, in the middle of the night, he came up with the perfect solution! He would make a lovely bag from jungle leaves, and fill it with berries for his friend to share at home. He would start weaving the bag the very next day. It would be a surprise for Crocodile!

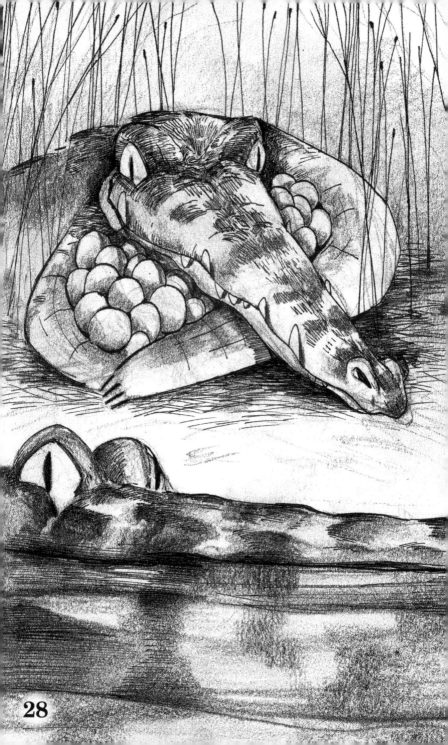

Meanwhile, Mrs Crocodile had come up with a plan of her own. The next time Crocodile returned without bringing her a single berry, she set her plan in motion.

'I'm tired of eating fish. Every day all I eat is raw fish. If I can't have something sweet, I will stop eating. I will get so thin that I will disappear. Then who will look after all our forty babies?'

'But what can I do, wife?' said Crocodile. 'I can't help swallowing when the berries are in my mouth.'

'You can bring me Monkey to eat,' his wife responded. 'He lives on berries so he must be as sweet as they are.'

Crocodile was horrified. 'Wife, you can't eat Monkey! He's my best friend.'

Looking pointedly at their forty eggs she said, 'I must have something sweet and that's an end to it. And,' she added cunningly, 'just think how fat Monkey is. There will be enough for us to share. Imagine how delicious he will taste!'

Crocodile did not want to imagine eating
Monkey. He tried not to imagine it, but his wife
kept on about how sweet Monkey would taste.
He looked at their nest and he thought about
sweet meat. At last, he agreed.

The next day, Crocodile swam over
to Monkey at the usual time. He did not
know that Monkey had spent the morning
filling the beautiful new pouch with berries.
Monkey planned to give him the pouch
when he was going home. But suddenly
Crocodile exclaimed, 'Listen! My wife is
calling me because the eggs are hatching!
She says I must bring you to meet our
forty children.'

'I didn't hear anything,' said Monkey.

'That's because she called me under the water. I heard her through my tail,' Crocodile lied.

'But how can I get there?' asked Monkey. 'You know I can't swim.'

'Just climb onto my back and wrap your tail around my neck and I will carry you,' said cunning Crocodile.

Monkey dropped on to Crocodile's back and his friend began to swim. The closer they got to his nest, the more slowly Crocodile swam. He hated the idea of eating Monkey. Who would listen to his problems? Who could he tell about the forty little crocs?

And so, as he always did, he told Monkey his problem.

Monkey did not like what he heard.
Nevertheless, he was a good friend, and as
always he used his clever brain to come up with
a solution for Crocodile.

'Crocodile,' Monkey said, 'you and your wife don't want to eat me.'

'I'm afraid we do,' said Crocodile, imagining how happy his wife would be when he brought her Monkey.

'If you eat me, who will pick you berries tomorrow, or any other day? I will be the last sweet thing you eat.'

'True,' Crocodile said. 'But I can't disappoint my wife or she will stop eating, and then my forty babies will have no mother.'

'I have a present for you and your wife back at my tree,' said Monkey, 'but we left in such a hurry that I forgot to bring it. If you take me back to get it, I promise our problem will be solved.'

'What present could solve a problem like this?' demanded Crocodile.

'I have spent all week making a big, beautiful bag. This morning I climbed to the top of the canopy and filled it with berries. If you take me back to my branch, I can give it to you and then your wife can have sweet berries today and every day.'

Crocodile swam back to Monkey's tree as fast as he could. Monkey leaped from his back and onto his branch and looked down at Crocodile. 'Friends don't lie to each other, Crocodile,' he said sternly. 'And they certainly don't eat each other! They talk to each other and they solve problems together. I've a good mind not to give you this present,' he said, holding the bulging bag of berries in his hands.

Crocodile hung his huge head in shame. 'You're right, Monkey. I don't know how I let myself be talked into betraying you. I promise I will never lie to you again. And I will never, ever harm you.'

While Monkey was thinking what to do, a cry rang out over the water (for of course, crocodiles do not hear with their tails). 'Crocodile, come home! The eggs are hatching!'

Monkey handed down the pouch. 'A birthday present for the forty babies and their mother,' he said.

'Climb aboard,' smiled Crocodile as he turned for home.

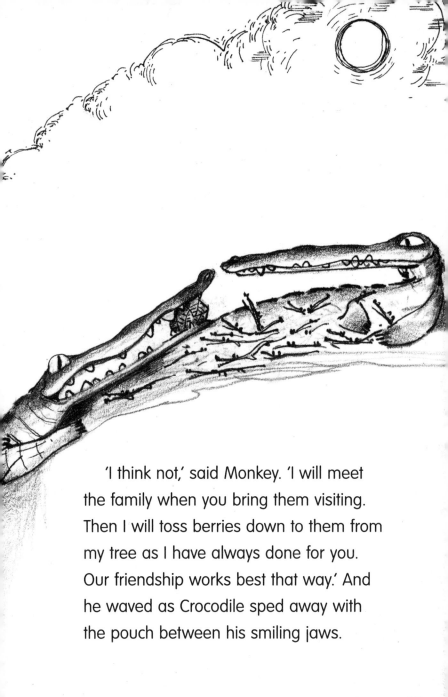

'I think not,' said Monkey. 'I will meet
the family when you bring them visiting.
Then I will toss berries down to them from
my tree as I have always done for you.
Our friendship works best that way.' And
he waved as Crocodile sped away with
the pouch between his smiling jaws.

The girl had stopped crying. She looked thoughtful. 'Does the story mean that I should find out why my friend tricked me?' she asked.

The storyteller nodded encouragingly. 'Now you are using your brain. Find out what's wrong and you can solve your problem together.'

The girl ran off happily.

Later in the day, the storyteller passed through the park again. She saw the two girls sitting on the swings. They were chatting and sharing some sweets as if they had never had a row. 'That's the use of stories,' she thought.

Storytellers are like stories; they are always travelling. The storyteller had spent several weeks in the town and had told many stories.

Sometimes she told them to one person, sometimes to many.

Adults listened thoughtfully and children
begged her for a new story whenever they
saw her.

'This is no longer a town without stories,' the storyteller thought with satisfaction.

It was time to move on.